in
the
news™

SUPERBUGS

THE RISE OF DRUG-RESISTANT GERMS

Stephanie Watson

ROSEN
PUBLISHING®

New York

This book is dedicated to all the medical heroes—the men and women who work tirelessly to find cures for what ails us

Published in 2010 by The Rosen Publishing Group, Inc.
29 East 21st Street, New York, NY 10010

Library of Congress Cataloging-in-Publication Data

Watson, Stephanie, 1969–
Superbugs: the rise of drug-resistant germs / Stephanie Watson.—1st ed.
    p. cm.—(In the news)
Includes bibliographical references and index.
ISBN 978-1-4358-3585-6 (library binding)
ISBN 978-1-4358-8553-0 (pbk)
ISBN 978-1-4358-8552-3 (6 pack)
1. Drug resistance in microorganisms—Juvenile literature. I. Title.
QR177.W38 2010
616.9'041—dc22

2009022964

5424
Manufactured in Malaysia

CPSIA Compliance Information: Batch #TWW10YA: For Further Information contact Rosen Publishing, New York, New York at 1-800-237-9932

On the cover: Clockwise from upper left: Gram-positive *C. difficile* bacteria cause many stomach ailments; antibiotic pills are used to treat bacterial infections; a hospital staff member puts on gloves to avoid spreading bacteria.

contents

What Are Superbugs?

Imagine an army of mutant invaders, billions strong. The members of this army are so tiny that they cannot be seen without a microscope. Their small size allows them to slip inside the human body, unnoticed. Once inside, they can cause sickness—even death. Nothing can combat these deadly invaders. They are unstoppable.

This scenario sounds like something out of a horror movie: "Attack of the Superbugs!" Although this description is overly dramatic, superbugs are real. Over the past few decades, bacteria have emerged that are resistant to all but the most powerful antibiotics. These bacteria can spread quickly through hospitals and communities. They make thousands of people sick each year. People whose immune systems aren't strong enough to fight off the bacteria can even die. Health experts fear that some day, strains of bacteria will arise that no medicine can kill.

Bacteria: Tiny Residents

Bacteria aren't really evil monsters. They are merely single-celled organisms that are trying to survive in the often-hostile environment of the human body.

It's true that bacteria can cause illnesses, such as pneumonia and strep throat. Yet many types of bacteria actually help humans become healthier. Many bacteria live in harmony within the body, serving useful purposes like keeping the digestive tract functioning properly.

For example, have you ever eaten a cup of yogurt with a label that read "Live Active Cultures"? Yogurt contains probiotics, which are bacteria that help make you healthier when you eat them. *Lactobacillus* and *Bifidobacterium* are the most common types of probiotics in yogurt. They take up residence in the digestive tract and help push out any harmful, disease-causing bacteria. Researchers have found that these good bacteria can help protect you from many intestinal woes, including diarrhea, gas, and constipation. People couldn't live without them. Other bacteria are used to produce antibiotics, which treat disease. In the environment, bacteria help break down garbage and other waste.

Bacteria are amazingly resilient organisms. They have been around for billions of years. They can survive in extremes of heat or cold that would quickly kill

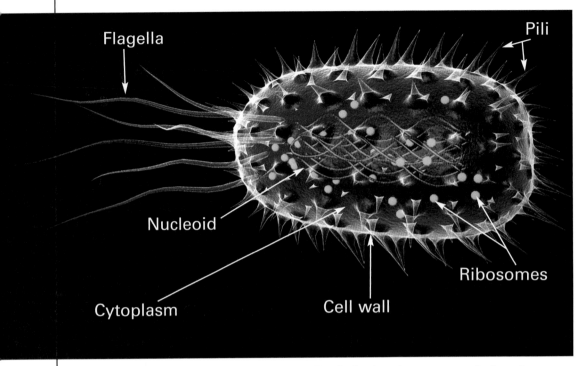

Bacteria are made up of a single cell. Their simple structure helps them survive in hostile environments.

humans or animals. Their simple design is what makes them so hardy. Because bacteria don't have complex bodies, they can adapt to just about any environment very easily.

It is important to mention that bacteria are not the same as viruses—the tiny microorganisms that cause the common cold and the flu. First of all, viruses are about ten to one hundred times smaller than bacteria. They cannot reproduce on their own like bacteria can. Illnesses caused by viruses cannot be treated with antibiotics. That is why when you have a cold, your doctor will prescribe lots of rest and fluids, but not antibiotics. In the past, doctors often mistakenly prescribed antibiotics for infections caused by viruses. That misuse of antibiotics is one of the reasons why some bacteria have become resistant to those drugs.

The Problem of Drug Resistance

Almost a century ago, scientists discovered a way to fight the bacteria that cause disease. The drugs that killed these germs were called antibiotics, and they worked pretty well. Bacteria are resourceful, though. They do whatever it takes to survive.

Over time, some types of bacteria changed. They developed ways to resist the effects of antibiotics. Some bacteria became more resistant to antibiotics than others.

Two types of bacteria exist: gram-negative and gram-positive. These names are based on how the bacteria react when they are colored by a technique called Gram's stain. The bacteria are first smeared on a slide and dyed with a purple stain. Then the bacteria are treated with an iodine solution. The iodine helps the dye attach to gram-positive bacteria. Finally, the bacteria are rinsed with ethyl alcohol. The alcohol washes the stain away from gram-negative bacteria, but the gram-positive bacteria stay purple and can be seen through a microscope. The last step in the Gram

The bacteria at top are gram-negative. They will turn pink from the second stain in the Gram's staining process. The bacteria at bottom are gram-positive. They turn purple when dyed with Gram's stain.

staining process is adding a second stain to turn the colorless gram-negative bacteria pink so that they can be seen under a microscope, too.

Gram-positive bacteria have only one membrane with a thick layer of peptidoglycan surrounding the cell. But gram-negative bacteria have two cell membranes, an inner membrane and an outer membrane, with a thinner layer of peptidoglycan in between. (The peptidoglycan is a macromolecule that serves a structural role in the bacterial cell wall.) In Gram's stain, the extra cell membrane of gram-negative bacteria makes it difficult for the dye to get inside and permanently stain the bacteria. That is the reason why they don't stay purple. This extra membrane also makes it more difficult for antibiotics to get inside the bacteria and kill them. That is one reason why many drug-resistant strains of bacteria are gram-negative.

When doctors try to treat infections with an antibiotic to which the bacteria are resistant, the medicine won't work. The patient will either stay sick for a long time or get even sicker. Very young children, elderly people, and those with a weakened immune system—for example, those who have the disease acquired immunodeficiency syndrome (AIDS)—are particularly vulnerable. They are more likely to die from drug-resistant bacteria.

Americans catch about two million infections in hospitals each year. More than 70 percent of these infections are resistant to at least one of the drugs commonly used to treat them, according to the Centers for Disease Control and Prevention (CDC).

Gram Positive

Plasma Membrane
Periplasmic space
Peptidoglycan

Plasma Membrane
Periplasmic space
Peptidoglycan
Outer membrane (lipopolysaccharide and protein

Gram Negative

The cell walls of gram-positive bacteria have only one thick membrane. The cell walls of gram-negative bacteria have two thinner membranes.

But before you panic, know that many health experts also say that very few healthy people are at risk from superbugs. Even if they are exposed to these resistant bacteria, most people have a strong enough immune system to fight them off.

Still, superbugs are a big problem. Doctors and researchers are looking for ways to stop them from becoming resistant to drugs. They are also developing new types of drugs that will kill even the most resistant bacteria.

The Superbugs 2

Any disease-causing bacteria have the potential to transform into superbugs. However, six types of bacteria are notorious for causing the most hospital infections and being the most antibiotic-resistant. Dr. Louis Rice, an expert in antibiotic resistance at the Louis Stokes Cleveland VA Medical Center in Cleveland, Ohio, came up with the acronym ESKAPE for these six deadly bacteria. ESKAPE stands for the following:

Enterococcus faecium
Staphylococcus aureus
Klebsiella pneumoniae
Acinetobacter baumannii
Pseudomonas aeruginosa
Enterobacter

Most of these bacteria probably sound foreign to you. Yet one has become a household name.

MRSA

Methicillin-resistant *Staphylococcus aureus*—or MRSA, as it is usually known—is by far the most famous superbug. Though staph usually starts out as a simple skin infection, it can transform into a serious illness. Strains of MRSA are resistant not only to the antibiotic methicillin but also to its cousins, penicillin, oxacillin, and amoxicillin.

A micrograph shows methicillin-resistant *Staphylococcus aureus* (MRSA) bacteria, the most notorious superbug.

MRSA isn't always dangerous, however. Between 25 and 30 percent of all people carry MRSA harmlessly inside their noses and mouths, and under their arms. Most of these people never get sick. Yet there are deadly strains of MRSA.

MRSA usually sneaks inside the body through an open cut. It tends to spread through hospitals, where there are many open wounds and injuries. A patient will come in carrying the infection, and it can easily jump from person to person, especially if the hospital and its staff don't keep everything perfectly sterile. People who are infected with MRSA can develop serious skin infections or tissue damage. The bacteria can also cause bloodstream infections (sepsis), pneumonia, and an infection of the brain and spinal cord (meningitis). In 2005, MRSA led to ninety-four thousand infections. Out of those, more than nineteen thousand people died, according to the CDC.

At one time, MRSA was only found in hospitals among elderly and very sick patients with poorly functioning immune systems. These types of infections are called hospital-acquired MRSA. Then cases began popping up in communities. In 2007, three children died from community-associated MRSA infection in New Hampshire, Mississippi, and Virginia. All the children had been healthy. The spread of MRSA among people who aren't sick or hospitalized has doctors and scientists very worried.

MRSA can even infect the biggest, strongest athletes. In 2003, eight players from the Saint Louis Rams football team contracted MRSA. That same year, linebackers Junior Seau of the Miami Dolphins and Ben Taylor of the Cleveland Browns had to be hospitalized because of the illness. Taylor developed MRSA after getting a simple scratch on the elbow.

Locker rooms are fertile breeding grounds for bacteria, including MRSA, because people are in close quarters and sharing personal items, such as razors and towels. Add to that the scrapes and scratches from playing contact sports, and it's no wonder that bacterial infections run rampant.

These young athletes are learning how to protect themselves against locker-room transmission of MRSA and other bacteria.

Today, sports teams have become more aware of MRSA and are paying more attention to good hygiene as a result. They are more careful about cleaning wounds, laundering towels, and putting antibacterial soap dispensers in locker rooms to help prevent infection.

MRSA comes in different forms, or strains. The vast majority of community-associated MRSA infections are due to a strain called USA300. This strain is more likely than hospital-acquired MRSA to cause infections in healthy people. However, it is also less dangerous and is easier to treat with antibiotics.

The Rest of the ESKAPE Superbugs

MRSA is the best-known superbug, but it's far from the only one. The five other bacteria that make up ESKAPE are the following:

> ***Enterococcus faecium*** These gram-positive bacteria normally live in the intestinal tract. Two types of enterococci, *Enterococcus faecalis* (*E. faecalis*) and *Enterococcus faecium* (*E. faecium*), can cause infections of the stomach, urinary tract, and bloodstream. Although the *E. faecalis* species causes infections far more often, *E. faecium* are much more resistant to common antibiotics, such as ampicillin and vancomycin. To treat *E. faecium* infections, doctors are forced to use new drugs that haven't been studied well and may have serious side effects. *E. faecium* bacteria can also pass genes for resistance to drugs like vancomycin to the more deadly *Staphylococcus aureus*, increasing their antibiotic resistance.
>
> ***Klebsiella pneumoniae*** In 2000, doctors at New York University's Tisch Hospital discovered that a patient in the intensive care unit (ICU) was infected with a particularly dangerous strain of *Klebsiella*, a gram-negative bacterium.

No matter what type of antibiotic the doctors gave the patient, the infection would not go away. Even the strongest disinfecting cleaners like ammonia couldn't kill the bacteria on surfaces. Within a year, two dozen patients at the hospital had been infected. Almost half of them died.

Klebsiella pneumoniae lives in both humans and animals, and it can stay alive on such surfaces as countertops and hospital operating tables. Because the bacterium has a thick outer membrane, the white blood cells of the immune system have a tough time breaking through and destroying it. *Klebsiella pneumoniae* is so deadly because it travels into the lungs and destroys alveoli, the air sacs that allow people to breathe. To combat the outbreak, Tisch Hospital had to implement strict sanitation procedures. The hospital kept infected patients in isolation, and it required staff and visitors to wear gowns, masks, and gloves at all times. Finally, in 2003, the outbreak was over.

Acinetobacter baumannii Very sick hospitalized patients are usually the most susceptible to infection with these gram-negative bacteria. Doctors were surprised when they discovered

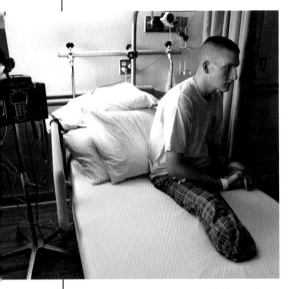

When this marine was injured in a roadside bomb explosion in Iraq, he became infected with the difficult-to-treat *Acinetobacter baumannii* bacterium.

that many young, healthy soldiers returning from combat in Iraq and Afghanistan had *Acinetobacter* wound infections. *Acinetobacter* infections are almost impossible to treat because they have become resistant to almost every antibiotic that is available. Doctors have had to resort to using very strong drugs with very serious side effects, including organ damage.

Pseudomonas aeruginosa Soil, water, and the bodies of animals and humans are all home to these rod-shaped, gram-negative bacteria. *Pseudomonas aeruginosa* are especially dangerous to very sick patients in the hospital because they cause serious infections of the heart, blood, brain, spinal cord, and lungs. Because *Pseudomonas aeruginosa* have become resistant to almost all antibiotics, doctors sometimes have to treat these infections with two antibiotics at once.

Enterobacter These gram-negative bacteria are found in the environment, as well as in the human intestinal tract. *Enterobacter* can cause serious infections of the urinary and respiratory tracts, especially in patients whose immune systems aren't working properly.

Other Superbugs

ESKAPE bacteria are the most common superbugs. But other types of bacteria are also becoming more drug-resistant. *Escherichia coli* (*E. coli*) bacteria have made headlines during outbreaks of infection linked to tainted spinach and beef. Meat and vegetables can become contaminated when they come into contact with animal feces. However, these strains of the bacteria typically aren't antibiotic-resistant. Most of the drug-resistant types of *E. coli* are found in hospitals and lead to urinary tract infections.

Clostridium difficile (*C. difficile*) are bacteria that produce toxins in the intestines, leading to severe diarrhea. In December 2005, researchers reported in the *New England Journal of Medicine* on a new and more potent strain of the bacteria that produces about twenty times more toxin than the regular strain. They say this drug-resistant strain emerged due to the use of antibiotics called fluoro-quinolones. The number of *C. difficile* infections in hospitals has jumped in recent years, and the infections are becoming more dangerous and difficult to treat.

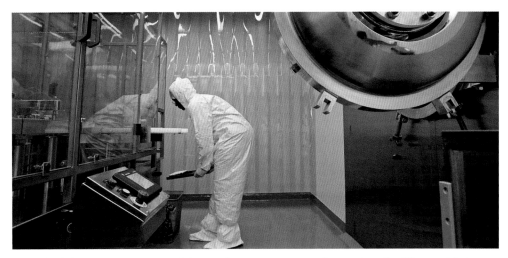

A technician operates machinery in a new manufacturing facility, which was built in Rockville, Maryland, to produce the tuberculosis vaccine.

Many diseases that were once treatable with antibiotics are now becoming drug-resistant. The deadly lung disease tuberculosis was nearly wiped out after the drug isoniazid was introduced in 1940. Today, doctors worldwide are seeing an increasing number of tuberculosis patients. In Great Britain, the number of tuberculosis cases has risen every year since the 1980s, according to a 2007 BBC News article. Old diseases like cholera, typhoid, and diphtheria are also coming back in harder-to-treat versions. Even basic childhood ear infections are proving more difficult to cure.

The genes that cause antibiotic resistance are spreading from one type of bacteria to another, leading to more and more drug-resistant strains. In the next chapter, you will learn how bacteria become resistant to antibiotics.

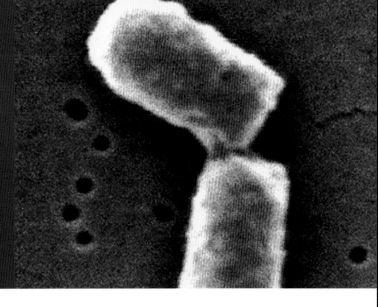

How Do Bugs Become Superbugs?

When antibiotics were introduced in the early twentieth century, doctors were thrilled to finally have medicine that could combat bacterial infections. They were so excited, in fact, that many of them began to prescribe antibiotics to treat just about anything, including colds and the flu, which are caused by viruses.

When people take antibiotics for colds and other viral illnesses, the drugs won't kill the viruses. Instead, the antibiotics will kill off some of the "good" bacteria in the body, leaving more room for harmful bacteria to move in and multiply.

Even when people take antibiotics for pneumonia, strep throat, or other bacterial infections, the bacteria can become resistant if the drugs aren't used properly. For example, if your doctor prescribes a ten-day course of amoxicillin and you take only five days' worth because you are starting to feel better, some of the bacteria in your body may still be alive. After having been exposed

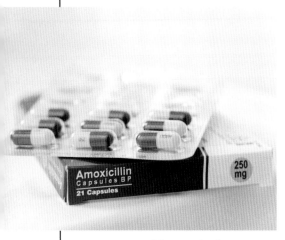

Many types of bacteria have become resistant to the antibiotic amoxicillin, which is pictured here in capsule form.

to amoxicillin, those bacteria can become resistant to the drug.

The idea of antibiotic resistance is based on naturalist Charles Darwin's idea of "survival of the fittest." Bacteria that are strong enough to resist the effects of the antibiotic survive to pass on their genetic traits to future generations of bacteria.

How Bacteria Evade People's Defenses

Bacteria are small, but they are resourceful. It is their very simplicity that makes them so hard to destroy. Antibiotics are designed to shut down many of the functions that keep bacteria alive. However, bacteria have developed very effective ways to evade these attacks.

Just like humans and animals, bacteria contain deoxyribonucleic acid (DNA), the genetic material that determines their characteristics. In humans, DNA determines such traits as hair color, eye color, and body shape. Groups of DNA called genes code for the production of various proteins in the body. These proteins determine how the body functions.

DNA has the ability to change, or mutate. In humans, mutations can lead to illnesses like cystic fibrosis and Huntington's disease. These mutations can be passed from parents to their children. The DNA in bacteria also mutates, but much more quickly and easily than in humans.

Genetic mutations can make the bacteria much stronger and better able to fight off antibiotics. When such a mutation occurs, those bacteria that have it will survive. Those that don't have the mutation will die off. Very quickly, the drug-resistant bacteria will start to take over the bacterial population.

Sometimes, bacteria acquire a new gene that enables them to begin producing a new type of enzyme (a protein with a chemical activity). Certain enzymes can damage the structure of an antibiotic so that the antibiotics no longer kill bacteria. For example, some strains of the bacteria *Staphylococcus epidermidis* produce an enzyme that makes penicillin ineffective.

Another possible genetic mutation helps the bacteria eliminate antibiotics more easily. Bacteria contain pumps (called efflux pumps) that remove toxic substances, including antibiotics, from their cells. A DNA mutation can cause the bacteria to produce a greater number of efflux pumps than normal so that the cell can pump out antibiotics more efficiently. *Pseudomonas aeruginosa* have a pump in place that can remove fluoroquinolones,

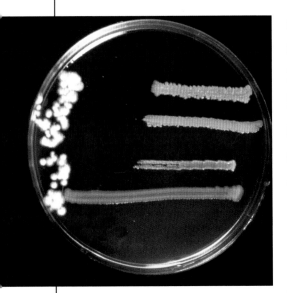

Penicillium notatum, a mold that produces beta-lactam antibiotics, is at the left in this petri dish. The bacterial strain at the bottom is able to keep growing because it is resistant to antibiotics.

a class of antibiotics used to treat many different kinds of infections. When bacteria with a large number of efflux pumps are exposed to fluoro-quinolones, the drugs are simply removed from the cells and the bacteria are not harmed.

Genetic mutations can help bacteria resist the effects of antibiotics in other ways as well. They can remove the target inside themselves that the antibiotics attack. Or they can strengthen their cell membrane so that the antibiotics cannot get inside.

Passing on Resistant Traits

Once bacteria have developed genetic traits for antibiotic resistance, it is very easy for them to pass those traits to other bacteria. One way is through a mating process in which the bacteria join up and directly pass their genetic information to each other. Bacteria can also pass their traits to a virus, which then injects the new gene for resistance into any bacteria that it attacks in the future.

Antibiotic resistance spreads through populations of bacteria in two ways: vertically and horizontally. Resistance spreads vertically when the gene is passed from one generation of bacteria to another. This can happen very quickly because bacteria reproduce with lightning speed. A single *E. coli* cell can replicate into millions of *E. coli* overnight.

Resistance spreads horizontally when bacteria share genes with each other. The genetic information needed to run a bacterial cell is housed in its chromosome—a double-stranded, circle-shaped piece of DNA. Sometimes, bacteria also contain a smaller free-floating piece of circular DNA called a plasmid, which contains a small amount of genetic information. Plasmids can transfer from one bacterium to another through a process called conjugation. During this transfer, the bacteria pass along the genetic instructions for antibiotic resistance.

This transfer can occur very quickly, causing a bacterial strain that was not drug-resistant to become resistant to antibiotics almost overnight. In 2003, the journal *Science* reported on the case of a patient with diabetes who had foot ulcers (sores) that had become infected with staphylococcus bacteria. The infection was proving difficult to treat with antibiotics. When doctors investigated, they discovered that many of the bacteria in the patient were resistant to some antibiotics, but a few were resistant to vancomycin, one of the most

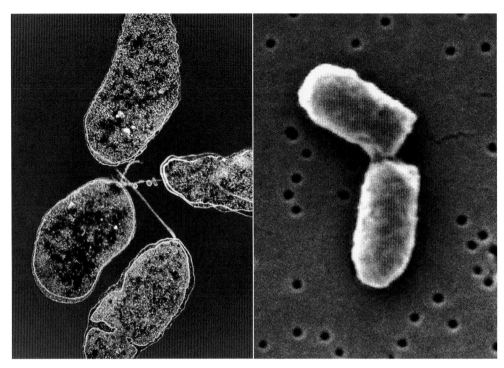

Left: These bacteria are exchanging their DNA through conjugation. Right: In this micrograph, bacteria are seen multiplying through cell division.

powerful antibiotics available. Did the bacteria mutate right inside of the patient's body? No. In fact, the doctors found traces of another type of bacteria, *Enterococcus faecalis*, which was already resistant to vancomycin. The gene for vancomycin resistance had literally jumped from one kind of bacteria (*E. faecalis*) to the staphylococcus bacteria. The gene made the staphylococcus resistant to vancomycin, too.

Bacteria that have developed genetic mutations protecting them from antibiotics can travel from place to place, introducing drug resistance to whole new geographic areas. People can also pass drug-resistant bacteria to one another when they are not careful about their hygiene.

Hospital Breeding Grounds

It is not surprising that superbugs were first spotted in hospitals, considering the large number of sick people and open wounds existing under one roof. Hospitals try hard to combat bacteria by cleaning surfaces with antiseptic cleansers, sterilizing surgical tools, and requiring doctors and nurses to wash their hands constantly. However, it is almost impossible for any hospital to be completely germ-free. That is why an estimated 85 percent of MRSA infections are contracted in hospitals and other health care centers, according to the CDC.

Germs have many modes of transportation into hospitals. Sick patients carry germs. Germs ride in on the clothes and shoes of employees and visitors. They are passed around when a nurse accidentally forgets to wash her hands or a doctor mistakenly uses the same stethoscope on two patients without cleaning it.

When they encounter the antiseptic world of the hospital, many bacteria immediately die. However, a few survive. By quickly copying themselves and

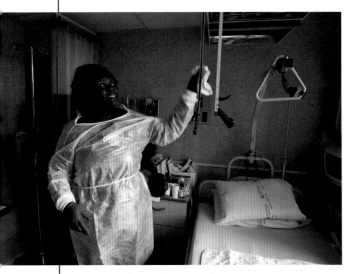

A hospital employee cleans a room with disinfectant to prevent the spread of MRSA.

passing their traits to other bacteria, antibiotic-resistant bacteria thrive.

In a hospital, it is very easy for drug-resistant bacteria to get inside of human bodies. They can enter through surgical cuts, catheters (tubes inserted in the body to inject drugs or remove fluids), or intravenous (IV) lines (tubes that send liquids or medicine directly into a vein).

Patients who are in the hospital are already sick. Many are very young or elderly, or have illnesses that make them weaker than usual. Their immune systems may not be strong enough to fend off a bacterial attack. That is why hospital-acquired drug-resistant infections can be so deadly.

Superbugs Throughout History

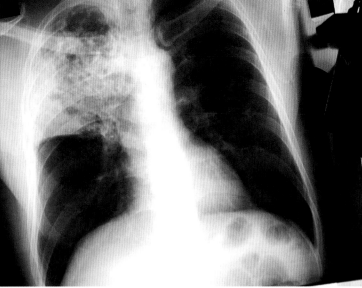

In the early twentieth century, parents feared their children's every cough or fever. There was always the chance that these were symptoms of an illness like scarlet fever, tuberculosis, or pneumonia. Surgery was also a frightening experience back then. A procedure as basic as having your appendix removed was often deadly. Any open wound became an easy entryway for millions of disease-causing bacteria. Without any effective medicines to combat bacterial diseases and infections, it was very common for people to die from these conditions.

Then in 1928, a young Scottish researcher named Alexander Fleming made an unusual discovery in his London laboratory. While doing an experiment, he smeared a culture dish with *Staphylococcus aureus* bacteria. Then he went on vacation for two weeks. When Fleming returned and looked at the dish, he noticed a yellow-green mold growing on it. Strangely enough, the mold seemed to be killing the bacteria.

Scottish researcher Alexander Fleming accidentally discovered what would become the world's first antibiotic— penicillin. Fleming is pictured here in his laboratory in 1955.

The mold was called *Penicillium notatum.* What Fleming had accidentally stumbled upon would form the basis of the world's first antibiotic, penicillin. About ten years later, a team of scientists at Oxford University in England were finally able to purify penicillin. When the researchers tested penicillin in animals and later in humans, they found that it was effective at treating bacterial infections, such as streptococcus. Soon, researchers figured out how to produce penicillin in large quantities.

New Antibiotics

The discovery of penicillin forever changed the way doctors treated bacterial infections. By the 1940s, penicillin was being mass-produced. The antibiotic was being used to treat pneumonia, scarlet fever, diphtheria, and many other infections. It was also helping prevent infections in soldiers wounded in World War II, as well as in patients undergoing surgery in hospital operating rooms. Penicillin was available to doctors everywhere, and it saved countless lives.

Scientists quickly followed up the discovery of penicillin with the introduction of several other types of antibiotics. In 1944, Rutgers University professor Selman A. Waksman discovered

A laboratory technician performs a test on the tuberculosis drug streptomycin in 1946.

streptomycin, the first real cure for tuberculosis. Other researchers figured out how to change natural antibiotics to make them more effective and how to produce synthetic (man-made) antibiotics.

Between 1940 and 1970, ten new classes of antibiotics were introduced. Each had a different target or method of action. In the 1980s and 1990s, researchers made improvements to classes of antibiotics already in existence. However, they didn't produce any new classes. Pharmaceutical companies had discovered that it wasn't worth the effort to produce drugs that people take for only ten days. They could make far more money producing medications that people take for many months or years, such as drugs for high cholesterol or heart disease.

The Growing Problem of Antibiotic Resistance

In 1969, U.S. surgeon general William H. Stewart announced in an address to Congress, "It is time to close the book on infectious diseases. The war against pestilence is over." Doctors believed they had conquered bacteria. They were mistaken.

Even in the very early days of antibiotics, Fleming was worried about the possibility of bacteria becoming resistant to the drugs. When he was awarded the Nobel Prize for Medicine in 1945, Fleming warned in his speech, "It is not difficult to make microbes resistant to penicillin in the laboratory by exposing them to concentrations not sufficient to kill them, and the same thing has occasionally happened in the body." Fleming had discovered that when penicillin was given in smaller-than-effective doses, resistant strains of bacteria survived.

As doctors overprescribed antibiotics and patients often neglected to take their entire dose, the problem of resistance grew. During World War II, penicillin was used for everything from treating pneumonia to preventing infections on the battlefield. Bacteria quickly became resistant to it. Researchers eventually developed partly synthetic forms of penicillin, such as methicillin. However, bacteria also became resistant to these drugs within just a few years.

Bacteria weren't just becoming resistant because of antibiotic use in medicine. Low doses of antibiotics were being put to other uses. They were added to cleaning products. They were fed to livestock to protect them from getting sick and help them grow faster. The more exposure bacteria had to antibiotics, the more their resistance grew.

Doctors began noticing that they were having more difficulty treating infections that were once easily curable with antibiotics. Between 1972 and 1992, New York City faced a major epidemic of drug-resistant tuberculosis. Tuberculosis is a disease that had almost been wiped out decades before. From the late 1980s to the early 1990s, the rates of tuberculosis infection tripled, according to the CDC. Many people who were infected died. It cost the city about $1 billion to finally stop the epidemic.

Many of the drug-resistant infections in the 1970s and 1980s were among people who were already sick. However, in the early 1990s, doctors began seeing strains

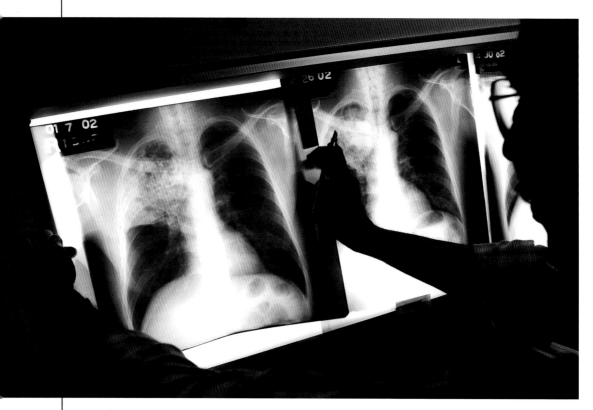

A doctor looks at X-rays of a tuberculosis patient in New York, where cases of drug-resistant tuberculosis were once on the rise. Tuberculosis is a disease that mainly affects the lungs.

of drug-resistant infections in people who were not sick. Robert Daum, the head of infectious diseases at the University of Chicago Children's Hospital, noticed that many otherwise healthy children were being admitted to the hospital with severe staph infections of the bone and skin. These staph infections did not respond to antibiotics. Many of the infections were life threatening. Superbugs were moving from hospitals into the general community.

Antibiotic Resistance in a Place Without Antibiotics

Scientists know that bacteria can become resistant when they are exposed to antibiotics. Yet they have discovered some bacteria that have become resistant without any such exposure. During the summer of 1968, Harvard University professor Robert Moellering was on a scientific expedition to North Malaita in the Solomon Islands, a remote group of islands in the southwest Pacific Ocean.

Moellering and his team of researchers took samples of bacteria from groups of native people and cultured (grew) them. On an island that had never had access to antibiotics, Moellering discovered bacteria that were resistant to the drugs streptomycin and tetracycline.

Superbugs have also been found in other parts of the world where there are no antibiotics. This evidence shows that overuse and misuse of antibiotics are not alone in causing antibiotic resistance. Some bacteria can become resistant to antibiotics on their own.

Superbugs Today

The problem of antibiotic resistance is not going away. It may be getting worse. In recent years, researchers have noticed a rise in the number of infections that don't respond to many common antibiotics.

In 1974, only 2 percent of staph infections were resistant to the common antibiotic methicillin. Today, more than 60 percent of staph strains (MRSA) cannot be treated with this antibiotic, according to a 2007 story on CNN.com.

Superbugs are also moving from hospitals to the community. Today they can be found wherever people are in close contact with one another, such as locker rooms, prisons, and schools, among other places. Whereas once they affected only sick people, superbugs can now affect healthy people, too.

Doctors and other health experts are very concerned about the rise of superbugs. Bacteria are becoming resistant to drugs faster than new antibiotics can be developed. However, that doesn't mean drug-resistant bacteria can't be treated. In the next chapter, you will learn about new ways researchers are finding to combat superbugs.

5
New Treatments

A ntibiotics work by interfering with the cell processes that keep bacteria alive. For example, the drug vancomycin blocks the production of the peptidoglycan that gives strength and shape to the bacterial cell. Other types of antibiotics may affect energy production in the bacteria or prevent them from multiplying.

Some antibiotics are effective against many different kinds of bacteria. These drugs are called broad-spectrum antibiotics. Levofloxacin and amoxicillin are examples of broad-spectrum antibiotics. Other drugs work against only a few types of bacteria. These drugs are called narrow-spectrum antibiotics. Penicillin and vancomycin are examples of narrow-spectrum antibiotics. Further, vancomycin is used just for gram-positive bacteria.

Although many antibiotics target both gram-positive and gram-negative bacteria, gram-negative bacteria are harder to treat because they have an extra membrane that makes it more difficult for drugs to penetrate the

Some Common Antibiotic Classes

Class of Antibiotic	How They Work	Effective Against
Aminoglycosides (streptomycin, amikacin)	Block protein production in bacteria	Gram-negative and a few gram-positive bacteria (*Pseudomonas, Acinetobacter, Enterobacter,* staphylococci)
Carbapenems (imipenem, meropenem)	Block formation of bacterial peptidoglycan	Gram-positive and gram-negative bacteria (streptococci, *Pseudomonas, Klebsiella*)
Cephalosporins (cefepime)	Block formation of bacterial peptidoglycan	Gram-positive and gram-negative bacteria (streptococci, enterococci, *Pseudomonas, Klebsiella*)
Fluoroquinolones (ciprofloxacin)	Interfere with DNA replication	Gram-positive and gram-negative bacteria (streptococci, *Pseudomonas, E. coli, Enterobacter*)
Macrolides (erythromycin, azithromycin)	Block protein production in bacteria	Gram-positive bacteria (*Chlamydia,* streptococci)
Penicillins (penicillin, ampicillin, amoxicillin)	Block formation of bacterial cell wall	Gram-positive and some gram-negative bacteria (streptococci, staphylococci, *Neisseria meningitidis*)
Tetracyclines	Block protein production in bacteria	Gram-positive and gram-negative bacteria (streptococci, *E. coli*)

Table adapted from the Sanford Guide to Antimicrobial Therapy *(2007)* cell. Both gram-positive and gram-negative bacteria are getting more difficult to treat because they are becoming resistant to the available drugs.

Doctors are finding they have fewer and fewer antibiotics that they can use to treat infections. As bacteria become resistant to common antibiotics like methicillin, doctors must turn to stronger drugs, such as colistin and linezolid. However, these antibiotics can have severe side effects. The worry is that bacteria will eventually become resistant to even the most powerful antibiotics in existence.

New Drugs for Superbugs

Although there are a few new antibiotics being developed, their numbers are very limited. Out of the eighty-nine new drugs approved by the U.S. Food and Drug Administration (FDA) in 2002, none were antibiotics, according to the 2004 report "Bad Bugs, No Drugs," by the Infectious Diseases Society of America.

Only a handful of new antibiotics have been introduced in the last few years, and some haven't been completely successful. In 2000, the FDA approved linezolid. It was the first in a new class of antibiotics to treat MRSA, hospital-acquired pneumonia, and blood infections. However, just four years after linezolid was introduced, bacteria started becoming resistant to it. In

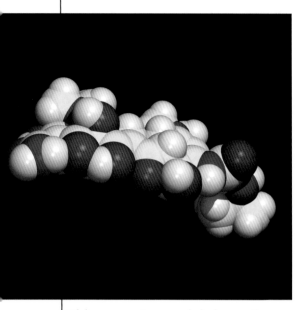

This computer model shows the antibiotic tigecycline, the first drug in a new class of antibiotics designed to treat MRSA and other superbugs.

2005, the FDA approved tigecycline. It was the first drug in another new class of antibiotics designed to kill the superbugs. Tigecycline seems to work well against very resistant bacteria. However, there are already *Acinetobacter* strains that are resistant to it.

Why are so few new antibiotics being introduced? A new antibiotic can take ten years and $800 million to develop, according to an article in the October 29, 2007, issue of *BusinessWeek*. Drug companies don't want to invest a lot of money in antibiotics because they don't earn big profits. People take antibiotics for just ten days. By comparison, they take drugs to treat long-term conditions, such as heart disease and high blood pressure, for many months or even years.

The longer people take a medicine, the more money the drug company earns. In 2003, the pharmaceutical company Cubist introduced a new and powerful antibiotic called Cubicin (daptomycin) to treat MRSA infections. The company earns approximately $500 million per year from selling the drug. In 2006, the drug company Pfizer earned an estimated $13 billion for its cholesterol-lowering drug Lipitor.

The money available for medical research on superbug treatments is also low. Funding by the National Institutes of Health (NIH) for research efforts to study ways of reducing bacterial resistance is just $35 million.

Even if there were enough money available, it is difficult for researchers to study bacterial resistance. As soon as people are admitted to the hospital with superbug infections, they are started on treatment. There are no control groups of patients on which to compare the results. Considering all of the challenges involved in studying drug-resistant bacteria, some research teams have had to come up with creative ways to tackle the problem.

Learning About Superbugs from the Inside

How do scientists learn what makes superbugs so super? Two scientific teams have found unique ways to find out exactly how drug-resistant bacteria operate.

At the University of Bradford in England, researchers have created an enclosed, climate-controlled bunker that contains exact replicas of real hospital wards. A research team made up of doctors, engineers, and other specialists is using this simulated environment

This researcher is among those at the University of Bradford in England who have created one of the world's largest controlled experiments in which to study superbugs.

to study how infections become resistant and spread.

Researchers at the London Centre for Nanotechnology have taken a different approach to studying superbugs. They are using levers as thin as a human hair to find out how vancomycin, one of the strongest antibiotics available, attacks bacteria. They've found that when vancomycin attaches to bacteria, it creates stress that breaks down the bacteria's peptidoglycan. Superbugs contain a tiny change in their genes that makes it about a thousand times more difficult for the antibiotic to attach to and disrupt the cell wall. Understanding how vancomycin harms bacteria could help researchers discover new and more effective bacteria-fighting drugs in the future.

Beating Bacteria at Their Own Game

Scientists are still trying to develop new antibiotics and make the existing antibiotics more effective. The problem is that bacteria have become pretty good at evading antibiotics. So researchers are taking a new approach. They are looking into ways to outsmart the bacteria.

One way that scientists are trying to outwit bacteria is by making drugs, such as the experimental antibiotic ceftobiprole, that are not destroyed by enzymes that make bacteria drug-resistant. In studies, ceftobiprole was able to kill even the most deadly strains of MRSA because the bacteria can't destroy it. The drug also killed strains of bacteria that were resistant to the powerful antibiotic vancomycin.

Another method being investigated is a way to strip bacteria of their ability to cause illness. That way, bacteria could live inside the human body without making people sick. For example, researchers are studying the communication system that helps bacteria cells "talk" with one another and with their host (the human body). This system lets bacteria know if they are in the right place in the body to cause infection. Scientists hope to target this system with new drugs that will hopefully stop the bacteria from communicating and causing damage.

Other new treatments being investigated include the following:

Superbug vaccines Vaccines work by teaching the body's immune system to fight off infection. Today's vaccines can protect against diseases like measles, mumps, and tetanus. In the future, a vaccine might be able to protect people against superbugs in the same way. In 2006, researchers were able to vaccinate mice against four different strains of MRSA.

Viruses vs. bacteria Both bacteria and viruses can cause illness in humans. Yet one type of virus is a friend to humans because it kills bacteria. These viruses are called bacteriophages, a word that literally means "to eat bacteria." Bacteriophages get inside of the bacterial cell, copy themselves, and then burst back out of the cell to infect other bacteria. In the process, they kill their host bacteria.

Komodo dragon saliva The Komodo dragon is the world's largest lizard. This fearsome creature can reach lengths of 10 feet (3 meters) and can weigh up to 300 pounds (136 kilograms). It turns out that Komodo dragon spit is also fearsome. The thick and gooey saliva is full of bacteria that quickly kill any animal that the dragon bites. Yet the dragon can live harmoniously with these deadly bacteria in its mouth. Researchers believe the Komodo dragon's drool contains natural antibiotics that protect it from the harmful bacteria. Now

The saliva of the Komodo dragon, which is teeming with deadly bacteria, could help scientists develop new antibiotics to protect humans from superbug infections.

they are trying to identify these substances and possibly use them to make a new type of drug to protect humans.

Scientists haven't yet found the "magic cure" that will wipe out superbugs. However, they are making great progress in investigating new treatments. Until these new therapies become available, people need to take precautions to help prevent superbugs.

Can Future Superbugs Be Prevented?

The news that more and more bacteria are becoming resistant to antibiotics sounds terrifying. Also frightening is the idea that one day, there might not be a single effective drug left to treat superbug infections.

The situation isn't hopeless, though. There are many easy ways to prevent the spread of drug-resistant bacteria. Some hygiene methods are implemented by hospitals. Others can be put in place right in your own home and school.

Hospital Screening and Hygiene

Hospitals were the birthplace of the superbugs, and they continue to pose a major risk for drug-resistant infections. Between 1999 and 2006, the number of patients with MRSA increased eightfold, according to an article in the February 16, 2009, issue of *AMNews*. Most patients pick up MRSA while in a hospital or other health care facility. To help combat superbugs, many hospitals have put infection prevention policies in place.

Some hospitals require that all patients be screened for MRSA and other superbug infections when they are admitted. To screen a patient, a health care worker rubs a cotton swab in the patient's nose to pick up any bacteria. The swab is then cultured in a laboratory to see if any bacteria grow. Patients who test positive are put in special isolation rooms until they test negative for the bacteria. Screening patients this way costs far less than the estimated $30 billion spent each year to treat super-bug infections, according to a 2007 article in *Scientific American*.

There is real evidence that hospital screening can reduce the rate of superbug infections. In one experiment, three hospitals in the Chicago area screened all of the patients entering their intensive care units. The hospitals discovered that MRSA infections dropped by 36 percent. Then the hospitals started screening every single patient who was admitted. MRSA infections dropped by 70 percent, according to a study in the March 18, 2008, issue of *Annals of Internal Medicine*.

In 2003, Allegheny General Hospital in Pittsburgh, Pennsylvania, implemented new procedures requiring staff to wash their hands and wear hospital gowns and gloves. The hospital trained all of its employees and then monitored them to make sure that they were

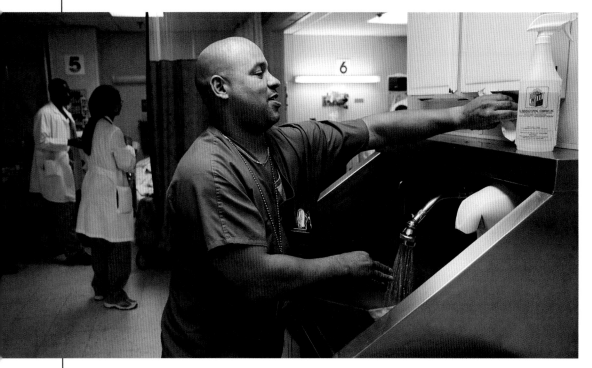

Requiring doctors and nurses to wash their hands regularly is one way in which hospitals are helping to cut down on the number of superbug infections.

following the procedures exactly. Within one year, Allegheny General Hospital was able to cut its bloodstream infections by 90 percent.

Even the simplest cleanliness measures can make a big difference. Doctors and nurses can help prevent the spread of infections just by washing their hands with soap and water after seeing each patient. Yet according to the *Scientific American* story, only about half of health care workers regularly wash their hands.

In an effort to reduce infections, many hospitals have started requiring their employees to practice good hygiene. At some hospitals, doctors and nurses have to wear gloves and change them after each patient. The hospital staff may be required to clean all surfaces, instruments, and equipment with bacteria-killing disinfectants between patients. Doctors may even be asked not to wear neckties because a tie can touch an infected patient and then pass the bacteria on to other patients that it touches.

Laws and Regulations to Prevent Superbugs

The problem of superbugs has become so widespread and serious that some states have actually passed laws to help curb the spread of infection. One type of law requires hospitals to screen patients for MRSA and other infections when they are admitted to the hospital. As of 2009, California, New Jersey, Illinois, and Pennsylvania had laws in place requiring all of their hospitals to screen patients. Several other states were considering enacting similar laws.

Another type of law requires hospitals to report their infection rates to the state department of health. Then the state publishes this information, letting consumers know which hospitals have high rates of infection. At least nineteen states, including Colorado, Connecticut, Delaware, Florida, South Carolina, and Oregon, have passed laws requiring hospitals to report infection rates.

Some states fine hospitals as much as $1,000 per day for not following the law.

Superbugs are not just an issue in the United States. Many other countries have passed strict laws designed to reduce their rates of superbug infections. Countries throughout Europe have banned farmers from giving the drug avoparcin to animals to help them grow because avoparcin is very similar to the antibiotic vancomycin. In Great Britain, every hospital is required to hire a director of infection control. This person is in charge of investigating and controlling the spread of drug-resistant bacteria. Countries in the Netherlands and parts of Scandinavia require strict hospital screening and hygiene practices, which have helped to keep their MRSA rates very low.

What You Can Do to Prevent Superbugs

Fighting superbugs starts with you. Stay healthy, practice good hygiene, and encourage your friends and family to do the same.

Keep clean. Good hygiene is essential for preventing superbugs. Wash your hands throughout the day with warm water and soap. To make sure that you have washed for a long enough time, don't turn off the water until you have finished singing "Happy Birthday" twice. If you don't have access to a sink, carry an alcohol-based hand sanitizer with you. Also wash any open cuts or scrapes with soap and water, and keep them covered with a clean bandage. Always wash your hands after handling raw meat, poultry, and fish. Raw foods can transmit *E. coli* and other types of bacteria, such as *Salmonella* and *Listeria*.

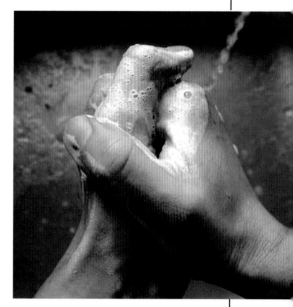

Thoroughly washing your hands with soap and water frequently during the day can help you reduce the chance of getting sick.

Don't share. When you were little, your mother probably taught you to share. But some personal items are not meant to be passed around. Keep your toothbrushes, razors, combs, and towels to yourself, and don't borrow these items from anyone else.

Take good care of yourself. Do everything you can to avoid getting sick. Eat a well-balanced diet, get at least eight hours of sleep each night, and try to stay away from anyone who you know is sick. When you are feeling under the weather or worn out, stay home and take a day or two off to recuperate.

Limit antibiotics. Don't rush to your doctor asking for antibiotics every time you have a cough or sore throat. The overuse of antibiotics has played a big part in the development of superbugs. Often, illnesses are caused by viruses, which aren't treatable with antibiotics. If you are worried that your doctor is prescribing antibiotics too often or for the wrong kinds of illnesses, ask him or her to take a culture to find out for sure if you actually have a bacterial infection. When you do have to take antibiotics, make sure to take the entire prescription. Stopping your medicine early can cause bacteria that are already in your body to become resistant.

Get more "friendly" bacteria into your system. Eat yogurt labeled with the words "Live Active Cultures." These probiotics will put more "good" bacteria into your body, crowding out the harmful bacteria.

Watch for the warning signs. The first symptoms of MRSA are easy to overlook. So easy, in fact, that many people don't know they are infected until the infection has become very serious. MRSA starts as small sores that look like pimples, boils, or spider bites. If you have a sore that is not healing, call your doctor.

Spread the news. Get your family, teachers, and classmates involved. Share with them what you have learned in this book. And encourage them to practice healthy hygiene, too.

Finally, be careful—but don't be paranoid. You don't need to live in fear that the superbugs are "coming to get you." Know that there is very little chance of you or

Regularly eating yogurt that contains probiotics can put more "good" bacteria into your body, leaving less room for harmful bacteria to multiply. Many people believe that eating probiotic food can ease digestive discomfort.

anyone you know getting sick with one of these infections. If you pay attention to good hygiene, your risk will be even slimmer.

What Will the Future Hold for the Superbugs?

What will happen to the superbugs depends on whom you ask. Some scientists fear that bacteria might one day become resistant to every type of drug available. They say that total bacterial resistance would mark an early end to the antibiotic era, which began with the discovery of penicillin in the early twentieth century.

Other people are much more hopeful. They believe that researchers will come up with a way to stop drug-resistant bacteria forever. They envision a future in which there are no more superbugs.

The reality is somewhere in between these two scenarios. Researchers are developing new drugs to kill bacteria. Hospitals are putting new policies in place to prevent bacteria from becoming resistant and stop the spread of bacteria that are already resistant. Some news indicates that these methods may be working. For example, bloodstream infections caused by MRSA in hospital intensive care units have dropped by 50 percent in the last decade, according to a study published in the February 18, 2009, issue of the *Journal of the American Medical Association*.

For now, humans will have to coexist with superbugs. These drug-resistant bacteria won't disappear overnight. Scientists may be able to slow down the process of resistance, but they probably won't stop it anytime soon.

Glossary

antiseptic Relating to a substance that prevents infection by killing germs.

bacteriophage A type of virus that infects and destroys bacteria.

broad-spectrum antibiotic A kind of antibiotic that is effective against a wide range of disease-causing bacteria.

catheter A long, flexible tube that is used to deliver fluids into the body or remove fluids from the body.

cell membrane A thin layer around the outside of a cell that controls the movement of substances into and out of the cell.

chromosome A circular, double-stranded, threadlike piece of DNA in a cell that carries the genetic instructions for the organism.

community-associated infection An infection that is picked up outside of a hospital or health care setting, in the general community.

conjugation The transfer of genetic material directly from one bacterial cell to another.

cystic fibrosis An inherited childhood disease that causes a thick mucus to form in the lungs. Cystic fibrosis patients often have infections caused by drug-resistant bacteria.

deoxyribonucleic acid (DNA) The material in a cell that contains genetic information.

efflux pump A protein in the cell membrane that acts like a pore to remove toxic substances, including antibiotics, from inside the bacterial cell.

enzyme A type of protein that triggers chemical reactions.

gene Sequence of DNA that codes for a protein and therefore determines a trait.

gram-negative bacteria Bacteria that do not retain the purple dye used in a gram-staining test. They have two membranes, inner and outer, that envelop and protect the cell. There is a thin layer of peptidoglycan between the membranes.

gram-positive bacteria Bacteria that remain purple when dyed in a gram-staining test. They have one cell membrane that is surrounded by a thick layer of peptidoglycan outside.

hospital-acquired infection An infection that is picked up in a hospital or other health care setting.

Huntington's disease An inherited disease that gradually affects movement, speech, and the ability to think. It is caused by an inherited mutation in the DNA.

immune system A complex group of organs and cells that defends the body against infection and disease.

mutation A change to the DNA that produces a different characteristic. Some types of mutations can make bacteria resistant to antibiotics.

narrow-spectrum antibiotic A type of antibiotic that works against only a limited number of bacteria.

peptidoglycan A complex macromolecule that forms a tough structural network to protect the cells of bacteria from the environment. Gram-positive bacteria can be stained because the cell wall is mostly made of peptidoglycan. However, gram-negative bacteria cannot be stained because they have very little peptidoglycan.

plasmid A small, circular piece of DNA in the bacterial cell that carries some of the genetic information. Plasmids can easily transmit genes from one bacterium to another.

probiotics Beneficial bacteria found in the intestines and contained in some types of yogurt.

sepsis A bacterial infection of the blood.

strep throat A bacterial infection in the throat and tonsils, caused by streptococcal bacteria.

superbug A bacterium that has become resistant to the effects of antibiotics used to treat it.

tuberculosis An infection of the lungs caused by *Mycobacterium tuberculosis*, a bacterium that is resistant to many of the drugs used to treat it.

For More Information

Centers for Disease Control and Prevention (CDC)

1600 Clifton Road

Atlanta, GA 30333

(800) CDC-INFO (232-4636)

Web site: http://www.cdc.gov

The CDC is a government organization that tries to protect human health by helping prevent disease and injury.

Infectious Diseases Society of America

1300 Wilson Boulevard, Suite 300

Arlington, VA 22209

(703) 299-0200

Web site: http://www.idsociety.org

This organization represents doctors and researchers throughout the United States. Its aim is to improve public health through research, better patient care, and information.

Public Health Agency of Canada

1015 Arlington Street

Winnipeg, MB R3E 3R2

Canada

(204) 789-2000

Web site: http://www.phac-aspc.gc.ca/id-mi/index-eng.php

The Public Health Agency of Canada helps promote the health of Canada's residents. Part of its work centers on preventing the spread of infectious diseases.

U.S. Food and Drug Administration (FDA)

5600 Fishers Lane

Rockville, MD 20857

(888) INFO-FDA (463-6332)

Web site: http://www.fda.gov

The FDA helps ensure the safety of medicines used in the United States.

Web Sites

Due to the changing nature of Internet links, Rosen Publishing has developed an online list of Web sites related to the subject of this book. This site is updated regularly. Please use this link to access this list:

http://www.rosenlinks.com/itn/super

For Further Reading

Ballard, Carol. *From Cowpox to Antibiotics: Discovering Vaccines and Medicines*. Chicago, IL: Heinemann, 2007.

Favor, Lesli J. *Bacteria* (Germs! The Library of Disease-Causing Organisms). New York, NY: Rosen Publishing Group, 2004.

Friedlander, Mark P., Jr. *Outbreak: Disease Detectives at Work*. Minneapolis, MN: Twenty-First Century Books, 2009.

Goldsmith, Connie. *Invisible Invaders: Dangerous Infectious Diseases*. Minneapolis, MN: Twenty-First Century Books, 2006.

Goldsmith, Connie. *Superbugs Strike Back: When Antibiotics Fail*. Minneapolis, MN: Twenty-First Century Books, 2007.

Guilfoile, Patrick. *Antibiotic-Resistant Bacteria*. New York, NY: Chelsea House Publishers, 2006.

Herbst, Judith. *Germ Theory*. Minneapolis, MN: Twenty-First Century Books, 2008.

Kowalski, Kathiann M. *Attack of the Superbugs: The Crisis of Drug-Resistant Diseases*. Berkeley Heights, NJ: Enslow Publishers, 2005.

Lewis Tilden, Thomasine E. *Help! What Is Eating My Flesh? Runaway Staph and Strep Infections!* New York, NY: Scholastic, 2008.

Lokere, Jillian, ed. *Cells: An Anthology of Current Thought* (Contemporary Discourse in the Field of Biology). New York, NY: Rosen Publishing Group, 2005.

Scientific American, eds. *Germ Wars: Battling Killer Bacteria and Microbes* (Scientific American Cutting-Edge Science). New York, NY: Rosen Publishing Group, 2008.

Sherman, Josepha. *The War Against Germs* (Germs! The Library of Disease-Causing Organisms). New York, NY: Rosen Publishing Group, 2004.

Tocci, Salvatore. *Alexander Fleming: The Man Who Discovered Penicillin* (Great Minds of Science). Berkeley Heights, NJ: Enslow Publishers, 2002.

Yount, Lisa. *Antibiotics* (Exploring Science and Medical Discoveries). Farmington Hills, MI: Greenhaven Press, 2004.

Bibliography

Ballantyne, Coco. "Hospitals and Superbugs: Go in Sick . . . Get Sicker." *Scientific American*, October 18, 2007. Retrieved December 18, 2008 (http://www. sciam.com/article.cfm?id=hospitals-and-superbugs).

BBC News. "Tuberculosis Cases 'Are Rising.'" March 22, 2007. Retrieved February 14, 2009 (http://news.bbc. co.uk/2/hi/health/6479537.stm).

Burton, Deron C., Jonathan R. Edwards, Teresa C. Horan, John A. Jernigan, and Scott K. Fridkin. "Methicillin-Resistant Staphylococcus Aureus Central Line-Associated Bloodstream Infections in U.S. Intensive Care Units, 1997–2007." *Journal of the American Medical Association*, February 18, 2009, Vol. 301, pp. 727–736.

BusinessWeek. "Superbugs: Where Are the Wonder Drugs?" October 29, 2007. Retrieved February 14, 2009 (http://www.businessweek.com/print/magazine/ content/07_44/b4056077.htm?chan=gl).

Crawford, Dorothy H. *Deadly Companions: How Microbes Shaped Our History*. Oxford, England: Oxford University Press, 2007.

Gilbert, David N., Robert C. Moellering, Jr., George M. Eliopoulos, Henry F. Chambers, and Merle A. Sande. *The Sanford Guide to Antimicrobial Therapy*. 37th ed. Sperryville, VA: Antimicrobial Therapy, 2007.

Grady, Sean M. *Biohazards: Humanity's Battle with Infectious Disease.* New York, NY: Facts On File, 2006.

Häusler, Thomas. *Viruses vs. Superbugs: A Solution to the Antibiotics Crisis?* New York, NY: St. Martin's Press, 2007.

Infectious Diseases Society of America. "Bad Bugs, No Drugs." Retrieved February 17, 2009 (http://www.idsociety.org/Content.aspx?id=5558).

Lowy, Franklin D. "Secrets of a Superbug." *Nature Medicine*, December 2007, Volume 13, Number 12, pp. 1,418–1,420.

Macrae, Fiona. "Copper Door Handles and Taps Kill 95% of Superbugs in Hospitals." *Mail Online*, October 29, 2008 (http://www.dailymail.co.uk/health/article-1081359/Copper-door-handles-taps-kill-95-superbugs-hospitals.html).

Moran, Gregory J., Anusha Krishnadasan, Rachel J. Gorwitz, Gregory E. Fosheim, Linda K. McDougal, Roberta B. Carey, and David A. Talan. "Methicillin-resistant *S. aureus* Infections Among Patients in the Emergency Department." *New England Journal of Medicine*, August 17, 2006, Vol. 355, Number 7, pp. 666–674.

MSNBC.com. "Superbugs More Widespread Than Thought." June 25, 2007. Retrieved December 18, 2008 (http://www.msnbc.msn.com/id/19403351).

Netterwald, James. "Super Drugs for Super Bugs." *Drug Discovery & Development*, May 2008. Vol. 11, No. 5, pp. 20–24.

O'Reilly, Kevin B. "States Consider Requiring Hospitals to Screen for MRSA." *AMNews*, February 16, 2009. Retrieved February 18, 2009 (http://www.ama-assn.org/amednews/2009/02/16/prsb0216.htm).

Playfair, John. *Living with Germs*. Oxford, England: Oxford University Press, 2004.

Robicsek Ari, Jennifer L. Beaumont, Suzanne M. Paule, Donna M. Hacek, Richard B. Thomson Jr., Karen L. Kaul, Peggy King, and Lance R. Peterson. "Universal Surveillance for Methicillin-Resistant *Staphylococcus aureas* in 3 Affiliated Hospitals." *Annals of Internal Medicine*, March 18, 2008, Vol. 148, pp. 409–418.

Sachs, Jessica Snyder. "The Superbugs Are Here." *Prevention*, December 7, 2006. Retrieved December 18, 2008 (http://www.prevention.com/cda/article/how-to-beat/8beb7e643f803110VgnVCM10000013281eac____/health/conditions.treatments/infectious.diseases).

Science Daily. "How Superbug Staph Aureus Resists Our Natural Defenses." March 28, 2008. Retrieved December 18, 2008 (http://www.sciencedaily.com/releases/2008/03/080324113258.htm).

Index

About the Author

Stephanie Watson is an award-winning writer based in Atlanta, Georgia. She is a regular contributor to several online and print health publications, and she has written or contributed to more than two dozen books, including *Animal Testing* (Science and Society), *The Genetics of Obesity* (Understanding Obesity), *Fast Food* (What's in Your Food? Recipe for Disaster), and *Changing Life Through Science* (Biotechnology).

Photo Credits

Cover (top left) CDC/Lois S. Wiggs, photo by Janice Carr; cover (top right, bottom), pp. 26, 46 Joe Raedle/Getty Images; pp. 4, 6, 44, 49 Shutterstock. com; p. 8 (top) CDC/Dr. W.A. Clark; p. 8 (bottom) CDC/Don Stalons; p. 9 Wikimedia Commons; pp. 10, 18 Chip Somodevilla/Getty Images; p. 11 CDC/Janice Haney Carr/Jeff Hageman, M.H.S.; pp. 13, 16, 40 © AP Images; pp. 19, 24 (right) CDC/Evangeline Sowers/Janice Haney Carr; p. 20 © Gustoimages/Photo Researchers, Inc.; p. 22 © Biophoto Associates/Photo Researchers, Inc.; p. 24 (left) © Dr. Kari Lounatmaa/Photo Researchers, Inc.; pp. 27, 32 Spencer Platt/Getty Images, Inc.; p. 28 Peter Purdy/Hulton Archive/Getty Images; p. 29 Kurt Hutton/Hulton Archive/Getty Images; pp. 35, 43 Torsten Blackwood/AFP/Getty Images; p. 38 © Dr. Tim Evans/ Photo Researchers, Inc.; p. 51 Getty Images Publicity.

Designer: Tom Forget; Editor: Kathy Kuhtz Campbell;
Photo Researcher: Cindy Reiman